A+
books

WORLD OF COLORS

Mexico in Colors

by Ann Stalcup

Consultant: Colin M. MacLachlan
John Christy Barr
Distinguished Professor of History
Tulane University
New Orleans, Louisiana

Capstone press

Mankato, Minnesota

Purple paper covers a table during a Day of the Dead celebration. Mexican families honor the dead on November 1 and 2. Children snack on sugar skulls. Candles and marigolds guide spirits home.

Red embroidery decorates the clothing of the Huichol people. The Huichol are famous for their clothing, colorful yarn pictures, and beaded animal heads. They live in the mountains of western Mexico.

Gray Mayan pyramids stand tall above the rain forest in southeastern Mexico. The Mayan culture began about 4,000 years ago. Many Mexicans have Mayan ancestors.

Green iguanas live in Mexico's rain forests. They eat flowers and leaves. Some iguanas grow to be 5 feet (1.5 meters) long. Hard scales cover their rough skin.

Red chili peppers grow on small farms throughout Mexico. Chili peppers make foods spicy. Many farmers grow peppers and other foods to feed their families.

The Gulf of Mexico's shimmering **blue** water invites tourists to take a dip. Mexico's coasts are always warm, but mountain areas are cool.

Orange, **blue**, and **pink** paint decorates this row of Mexican homes. Families use bright colors to welcome visitors. Grandparents, parents, and children often share the same home.

A Mexican girl swings a stick at a **purple** piñata. Candy or small toys spill onto the ground when a piñata breaks. Many Mexicans celebrate Christmas and birthdays with colorful piñatas.

Aztec dancers in bright **green**, **pink**, and **yellow** costumes perform in a Mexico City plaza. Mexico City is the capital of Mexico. It stands on the same spot as the ancient Aztec capital. The Aztecs thrived in Mexico during the 1400s and 1500s.

Green peppers, red tomatoes, and oranges fill a Mexico City market stall. The peppers and tomatoes are chopped up and served with cooked beans and tortillas. Mexicans eat beans and tortillas with most meals.

A bullfighter twists his **red** cape to tease a bull. Many families enjoy watching bullfights. Most large cities in Mexico have bullrings.

Villagers in Oaxaca created these green and orange dream animals. They are carved from the soft wood of copal trees. These colorful animals are in museums around the world.

Mariachi players in **black** uniforms strum guitars and pluck violins. They create Mexico's most joyous music. Mariachi bands perform at parties and weddings. They even play while walking down the street!

FACTS about Mexico

Capital City: Mexico City

Population: 108,700,891

Official Language: Spanish

Common Phrases

English	Spanish	Pronunciation
hello	hola	(OH-la)
good-bye	adiós	(ah-dee-OSE)
please	por favor	(POR fah-VOR)
thank you	gracias	(GRAH-see-uhss)

Map

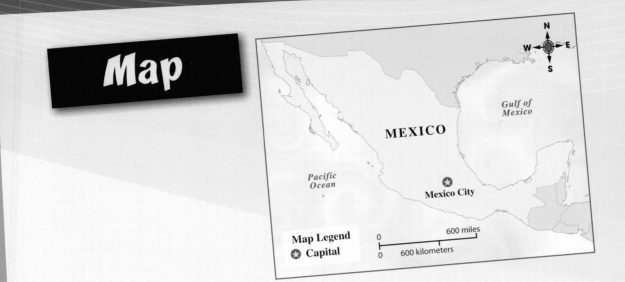

Flag

Money

Mexican money is called the peso. One peso equals 100 centavos.

Glossary

ancestor (AN-ses-tuhr) — a family member who lived a long time ago

Aztec (AZ-tek) — a member of an American Indian people who lived in Mexico before Spanish people settled there

embroidery (im-BROY-duh-ree) — a form of sewing used to sew pictures or designs on cloth

Huichol (WEE-chole) — a member of an American Indian people who lives in the mountains of Mexico

mariachi (mah-ree-AH-chee) — a Mexican street band

Maya (MY-uh) — a member of an American Indian people who lives in southern Mexico and Central America

Oaxaca (wuh-HA-kah) — a Mexican state; Mexico has 31 states.

piñata (pin-YAH-tuh) — a hollow, decorated container filled with candy or toys; a person tries to break the piñata with a stick.

pyramid (PIHR-uh-mid) — a stone monument

rain forest (RAYN FOR-ist) — a thick forest where a great deal of rain falls

tortilla (tor-TEE-yah) — a round, flat bread made from cornmeal or flour

Read More

Hodgkins, Fran. *Mexico: A Question and Answer Book.* Questions and Answers. Mankato, Minn.: Capstone Press, 2005.

Krebs, Laurie. *Off We Go to Mexico!: An Adventure in the Sun.* Cambridge, Mass.: Barefoot Books, 2006.

FactHound offers a safe, fun way to find Internet sites related to this book. All of the sites on FactHound have been researched by our staff.

Here's how:

1. Visit www.facthound.com

2. Choose your grade level.

3. Type in this book ID **1429617020** for age-appropriate sites. You may also browse subjects by clicking on letters, or by clicking on pictures and words.

4. Click on the **Fetch It** button.

FactHound will fetch the best sites for you!

Index

A+ Books are published by Capstone Press,
151 Good Counsel Drive, P.O. Box 669, Mankato, Minnesota 56002.
www.capstonepress.com

112009
005631R

Library of Congress Cataloging-in-Publication Data
Stalcup, Ann, 1935–
    Mexico in colors / by Ann Stalcup.
    p. cm. — (A+ books. World of colors)
    Summary: "Simple text and striking photographs present Mexico, its culture,
and its geography" — Provided by publisher.
    Includes bibliographical references and index.
    ISBN-13: 978-1-4296-1702-4 (hardcover)
    ISBN-10: 1-4296-1702-0 (hardcover)
    1. Mexico — Juvenile literature. [1. Mexico.] I. Title. II. Series.
F1208.5.S65 2009   2008005275
972 — dc22

Credits
Megan Peterson, editor; Veronica Bianchini, designer; Wanda Winch, photo researcher

Photo Credits
Alamy/Keith Dannemiller, 16–17 (girl); Ann Stalcup, 4–5; Art Life Images/age
fotostock/Henry Beeker, 8–9; Art Life Images/age fotostock/Jeronimo Alba, 22–23;
Art Life Images/age fotostock/Terrance Klassen, cover; Corbis/zefa/Hugh Sitton,
26–27; Getty Images Inc./The Image Bank/Walter Bibikow, 14–15; Houserstock/Jan
Butchofsky-Houser, 2–3; Peter Arnold/Ron Giling, 20–21; Shutterstock/Bobby Deal/
RealDealPhoto, 1; Shutterstock/Carolina K. Smith, M.D., 29 (coins); Shutterstock/
Danilo Ascione, 29 (banknote); Shutterstock/Douglas Knight, 11; Shutterstock/
jmatzick, 16 (piñata); Shutterstock/Luisa Amare, 12–13; South American Pictures, 25;
South American Pictures/Chris Sharp, 18–19; South American Pictures/Robert Francis,
6–7; StockHaus Ltd., 29 (flag)

Note to Parents, Teachers, and Librarians
This World of Colors book uses full-color photographs and a nonfiction format
to introduce children to basic topics in the study of countries. *Mexico in Colors*
is designed to be read aloud to a pre-reader or to be read independently by an
early reader. Photographs help listeners and early readers understand the text
and concepts discussed. The book encourages further learning by including the
following sections: Facts about Mexico, Glossary, Read More, Internet Sites, and
Index. Early readers may need assistance using these features.